D1597851

AMAZING HISTORY

SPIES AND TRAITORS

JAMES STEWART

A⁺

Smart Apple Media

Published by Smart Apple Media
2140 Howard Drive West
North Mankato, MN 56003

Created by Q2A Media
Series Editor: Jean Coppendale
Designers: Diksha Khatri, Ashita Murgai
Picture Researchers: Lalit Dalal, Jyoti Sachdev
Illustrators: Aamir Khan, Manish Prasad, Rajesh Das, Rishi Bhardwaj, Hemant Arya, Vijay R Sharma, Prashant Jogi

Picture credits
t=top b=bottom c=center l=left r=right m=middle
Cover: Images.Com/ Photolibrary: background, Nruboc/ Dreamstime.com: t,
Edyta Pawlowska/ Shutterstock: m, James E. Knopf/ Shutterstock: bl, Galina Barskaya/ Shutterstock: br.
Back cover: troy/ Shutterstock: tl, Carolina K. Smith, M.D./ Shutterstock: tm, Stephen Sweet/ Shutterstock: tr.
Stefano Bianchetti/ Corbis: 4b, Corbis: 5t, David Samson/ Corbis Sygma: 5b, Photolibrary.Com: 6b,
National Bibliothèque of France: 7b, The Bridgeman Art Library/ Photolibrary: 8b, 11t,
Science Photo Library/ Photolibrary: 9t, 28b, The British Library Board: 9b, The Library of Congress: 10b, 12b, 18b, 21b, 25t,
James Steidl/ Istockphoto: 11b, Leonard de Selva/ Corbis: 13b, Austin Mills: 14b, National Security Agency: 15t,
Q2A Media: 15b, 16t, 17t, 20br, 21t, 25b, 26bl, 26br, 27l, 27r, John McConnell: 16b, Ersler Dmitry/ Shutterstock: 17b,
Super Stock/ Dinodia: 19r, Imperial War Museum/ Crown Copyright: 20bl, Navy.mil: 22b,
Tim Ockenden/ PA Archive/ PA Photos: 23t, Movieposter.com: 23b, Bettmann/ Corbis: 24t,
Nasa: 24m, WizData/ Bigstockphoto: 28m.

Printed in China

The Library of Congress has cataloged the hardcover edition as follows:

Stewart, James, 1947–
Spies and traitors / by James Stewart.
p. cm. — (Amazing history)
Includes index.
ISBN 978-1-59920-109-2
ISBN 978-1-59920-210-5 (pbk)
1. Spies—Juvenile literature. 2. Espionage—Juvenile literature. 3. Traitors—Juvenile literature. I. Title.

UB270.5.S85 2007
327.12—dc22   2007023156

First Edition

9 8 7 6 5 4 3 2 1

Contents

Spies and traitors

Spies are really thieves. They steal and pass on top-secret information, using equipment such as hidden cameras, microphones, and recorders. They may work for a government, an organization, or an individual.

Spies have eyes

Throughout history, spies have been used to collect information about an enemy. In biblical times, Joshua, a leader of the **Israelites**, sent men to spy on the city of Jericho. When the spies returned, Joshua used their information to conquer the city and defeat his enemies.

HOT SPOTS

Ancient Egyptian pharaohs used a network of spies to watch their disloyal subjects and defeat their enemies. Egyptian spies were among the first to use secret **codes** *and trick inks.*

Joshua, in front of the collapsing walls of Jericho. Joshua sent spies into the city. They told him how many soldiers were in the city and what weapons they had.

The word "quisling" is now used all over the world to mean someone who is a traitor.

Nazi salute

Quisling giving a **Nazi** salute

Deadly traitor

Traitors **betray** their own country. Some, such as the Norwegian army officer Vidkun Quisling, work for the enemy. When the Germans invaded Norway in World War II, Quisling took their side. In 1942, the Germans made him Minister President of Norway. After the war, Quisling was arrested for **treason** and executed by a firing squad.

Spying for money

Some traitors give information in return for money. Spies and traitors demand huge sums for betraying their country. In 1985, CIA agent Aldrich Ames offered to work for the Russian KGB. He was paid $2.5 million for passing secrets.

In 1994, Alrich Ames was charged with treason and sentenced to life imprisonment.

5

Treason!

Treason is the crime of betraying one's country. Spies and traitors are guilty of treason—if caught, they are often executed.

Deadly plots

Around 45 B.C., Julius Caesar was the most powerful man in Rome. But some senators thought Caesar had become too powerful. Led by Brutus and Cassius, a group of traitors plotted Caesar's murder. On March 15, 44 B.C., the group surrounded Caesar as he was arriving at the Senate and stabbed him to death. This murder led to a civil war in which the traitors were hunted down and killed.

Julius Caesar was given the title Dictator of Rome for life. Because of his power, he had many enemies.

Perfect plot
The traitors hid knives in their togas

Backstabbers
Caesar was stabbed to death at the Senate in Rome

Storming the city

In 1095, Pope Urban II called on Christian soldiers to recapture the holy city of Jerusalem from the Muslims. These soldiers, called Crusaders, first had to take Antioch, a Syrian city defended by mighty towers and high walls. The Crusaders attacked for more than six months, but Antioch held out. Then, in May 1098, the Crusaders heard that a huge Muslim army was coming to save Antioch. Just before it arrived, a Crusader leader spoke to Firouz, the captain of one of the city's towers. Firouz became a traitor and agreed to open his gates to the enemy.

HOT SPOTS

*Ninjas were secret **assassins** and spies that were used by rulers in Japan between the ninth and twelfth centuries. They spied on their lords' enemies, stole their food, and took their weapons.*

The Crusaders made a deal with the traitor, Firouz, and he opened the gates of Antioch to let them in. The Crusaders captured the city with terrible bloodshed.

Plots against the Crown

Kings and queens have always had to defend themselves against plots and **conspiracies** to remove them from power. Many have used spies to unmask traitors working against them.

MARIE STVARD

The execution of Mary Queen of Scots was so badly carried out that it took three blows to cut off her head.

Super spymaster

Queen Elizabeth I of England had a network of spies to protect her from plotters. These spies were organized by a spymaster, Francis Walsingham. He discovered plots to kill Elizabeth and put her Catholic cousin, Mary Queen of Scots, on the throne. Walsingham paid Gilbert Gifford to act as a **double agent** to trap Mary. Gilbert smuggled coded messages, hidden in a beer barrel, from Mary to her supporters. These messages proved that she was guilty of treason. When Elizabeth read the **decoded** letters, she sentenced Mary to be beheaded.

HOT SPOTS

For many years, the British punished the crime of high treason by hanging, drawing, and quartering. Only men were executed in this way—women were burned at the stake.

The Gunpowder Plot

In 1605, a group of angry Catholics plotted to blow up the Houses of Parliament and kill King James I of England, who was a **Protestant**. Guy Fawkes, a soldier who knew how to use explosives, was chosen to do the deed. He filled a cellar under Parliament with 36 barrels of gunpowder. His plan was to blow them up on November 5, when the king was in the building above. The plot was discovered just in time.

The conspirators believed that when King James was dead, England would change from a Protestant country to a Catholic one.

The execution of Guy Fawkes and other plotters was done in the slowest, most painful way—by hanging, drawing, and quartering.

Hanged
But not long enough to kill

Drawn
The stomach and intestines were pulled out

Quartered
The body was dragged off and cut into four pieces

Revolution!

Spies and traitors sometimes helped in **revolutions**, when kings, queens, and governments were removed by violence. Occasionally, a single spy managed to change the course of history.

An American traitor

In 1780, during the **Revolutionary War**, when Americans were fighting to break free from British rule, the British officer John Andre came up with a wicked plan. He persuaded Benedict Arnold, the American general in charge of the fort at West Point, to hand it over to the British for £20,000. After making the deal, Andre set out for home with the plans of the fort hidden in his boots. Unfortunately for him, he was stopped and searched by American soldiers, who found the plans. Andre was hanged as a spy.

Spy in boots
Secret plans were hidden in Andre's boot

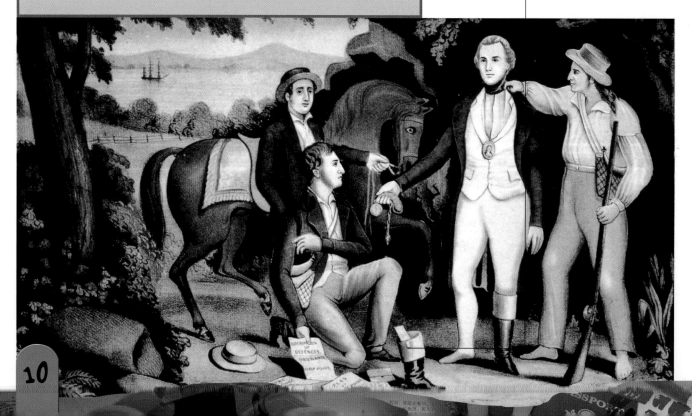

Major John Andre tried to disguise himself by wearing an American uniform. But he was captured by American soldiers who found Benedict Arnold's secret plans.

Joseph Fouché, head of Napoleon's secret police, kept his master in power but also plotted against him.

Minister of police

The years that followed the **French Revolution** of 1789 were full of trouble. Joseph Fouché did better than most by making sure he was always on the winning side. First, he voted in favor of the execution of **King Louis XVI** by the guillotine in 1793. Then, six years later, he helped **Napoleon Bonaparte** take power in 1799. Napoleon never trusted Fouché, but he needed the network of spies that he ran, so the spymaster survived. Fouché was so powerful that he even managed to keep his job after Napoleon's defeat in 1815.

Sharp blade
Cut off the person's head

In 1792, Doctor Joseph-Ignace Guillotine invented the guillotine as a quick and almost painless method of execution.

Assassination

Assassins are murderers who kill important people. Some are mad, but many are traitors. Their acts of assassination have often changed the course of history.

Theater tragedy

On April 14, 1863, President Abraham Lincoln was assassinated in a theater. His killer was John Wilkes Booth, an actor who blamed Lincoln for all of America's problems. While Lincoln was watching the play, Booth came up behind him and shot him in the head at point blank range. The president died early the next morning. Booth escaped from the theater but was later shot dead. At least four other people were involved in the plot to assassinate the president.

President Lincoln was shot behind his left ear. The bullet entered his skull and lodged behind his right eye—leaving him paralyzed and barely breathing.

Point blank
John Wilkes Booth used a single-shot, derringer pistol

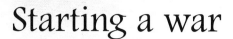

Starting a war

The world's most famous assassination took place on June 28, 1914. Austrian Archduke Franz Ferdinand was visiting Sarajevo, in Bosnia, when his driver took a wrong turn down a side street. By chance, the assassin Gavrilo Princip was in the same street. When the royal car stopped, Princip drew a pistol and shot both the prince and his wife. They died shortly after. Because Princip had ties to Serbia, Austria declared war on Serbia, which sparked a series of events that led to the outbreak of World War I.

After assassinating Archduke Franz Ferdinand and his wife, Gavrilo Princip tried to shoot himself and take cyanide, but he was captured by the police. He died in prison four years later.

Secret codes

Spies have always used secret codes to pass on information. **Intercepting** messages and breaking codes has become a vital role of the secret services.

New spies

During the Civil War (1861–65), both sides set up their own **spy rings**. For the North, Colonel George H. Sharpe set up the Bureau of Military Information. It used information from spies, prisoners of war, enemy newspapers, and even documents found on dead bodies on battlefields to write detailed reports about the enemy. Both sides used a new invention—photography—to record information. Messengers working for the South carried mini-photo messages hidden in hollow buttons.

THE CONFEDERATE CIPHER DISK
The Confederate cipher disk was made of brass. Only two and one-quarter inches in diameter, it was small enough to easily fit into a vest pocket. The device consisted of two disks with the smaller inner disk revolving on a central pivot. Each disk had the alphabet (reading left to right) imprinted around its circumference. The red letters SS are thought to stand for Secret Service. Only five original examples are known to exist.

Working for the Southern forces, the **Confederate** Signal Service Bureau used this cipher disk to create messages in secret codes.

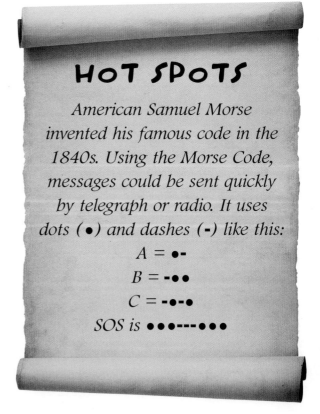

HOT SPOTS

American Samuel Morse invented his famous code in the 1840s. Using the Morse Code, messages could be sent quickly by telegraph or radio. It uses dots (•) and dashes (-) like this:

A = •-

B = -••

C = -•-•

SOS is •••---•••

Breaking codes

During World War II, the **Allies** worked hard to break enemy codes. The Germans had built a complicated machine to make codes. Called the Enigma, it used a system of gears, keys, and lights. The Germans believed codes made by the Enigma machine could never be broken, so they used it to transmit top-secret messages about their military operations. However, the brilliant British mathematician, Alan Turing, managed to break the Enigma code and read German messages. This gave the Allies a great advantage, shortening the war and helping to save many lives.

During World War II, the German Enigma machine used levers and electricity to scramble vital messages and information into a secret code.

Code keys
The message was keyed in

Alan Turing worked at Bletchley Park in Buckinghamshire. This was the British code-breaking center during World War II.

Enigma machine
Contained everything necessary to make codes

Secret services

Every country needs to defend itself against possible enemies. Its intelligence service helps do this by employing spy networks to gather and analyze information.

Intelligence services

The U.S. intelligence service is the Central Intelligence Agency (CIA). It works secretly to find out about foreign governments, people, and companies. Since 1947, the CIA has worked in many secret operations around the world—even planning assassinations. In Britain, **espionage** activities are carried out by the Secret Intelligence Service, also known as MI6. After World War II, the chief enemy of MI6 and the CIA was the secret service of the **Soviet Union**, known as the KGB.

The CIA badge showing the bald eagle, which is the national bird of the United States.

Thames House in London is the headquarters of MI6.

Sword and shield
The sword to strike enemies and the shield to defend the Russian revolution

Hammer and sickle
The symbol of the Soviet Union

The badge of the KGB (Committee for State Security). The KGB was the secret service of the Soviet Union from 1954 to 1991 and had nearly 500,000 employees.

HOT SPOTS
The Americans Aldrich Ames, John Anthony Walker, and Robert Hanssen all become KGB spies just by walking into the Soviet Embassy in Washington and offering their services. Each man earned millions of dollars for their espionage.

KGB agents

The much-feared KGB had its headquarters in Moscow. There were KGB spies, or agents, in many Western countries, especially the U.S. and the UK. KGB agents managed to steal the secrets of the atomic bomb, as well as detailed plans about radar and jet engines. The KGB was also helped to crush anti-Russian uprisings in Hungary (1956) and Czechoslovakia (1968).

The headquarters of the KGB, in Lubyanka Square, Moscow.

Deadly ladies

Throughout history, women spies have played a major part in espionage activities. Many of them became friends with the enemy in order to discover vital information.

Southern spy

Belle Boyd was a spy for the South, during the Civil War. Her spying career began in 1861, when she killed one of the Union (Northern) soldiers who had broken into her home. However, Belle was found not guilty of murder, and she used her friendship with Union soldiers to get information from them. In May 1862, listening through a hole in the floor of her room in her father's hotel, she learned their secret plans. Belle then rode through the night to tell Stonewall Jackson, the Southern commander, that it was safe to attack the Union forces in the Shenandoah Valley in Virginia. He took her advice and won the battle.

Belle was awarded the Southern Cross of Honor for her spy work.

The dancing spy

Mata Hari was born in Holland in 1876. During World War I, she became friends with high-ranking French army officers and told them she was working for French military intelligence. In 1917, the French intercepted German radio messages suggesting that Mata Hari was really spying for the Germans. She was put on trial, found guilty, and executed by a firing squad. Her last act was to blow a kiss to her executioners. Many books and films have since been made about her life.

Mata Hari, whose real name was Margaretha Zelle, was a very popular dancer in Paris before she was arrested for spying.

Firing squad
Mata Hari faced 12 soldiers with rifles

Facing death
Mata Hari refused to wear a blindfold or have her hands tied

Mata Hari was executed by a firing squad in 1917.

19

World War II

During World War II, the Soviet Union, the UK, Germany, and Japan relied on their powerful secret services. Many of their bravest men and women were killed while working as spies.

The bravest of all

After Violette Szabo's husband was killed in the war, the British Special Operations Executive (SOE) trained her as a secret agent. Born in France, she spoke perfect French, so it was easy for her to pretend to be a French person. In April 1944, she parachuted into France and helped the anti-German **resistance fighters** who were blowing up bridges. On her second mission to France in June 1944, she was captured by the Germans and tortured. Later, Violette was sent to Ravensbruck **concentration camp** where she was executed when she was only 23 years old.

Violette Szabo was awarded the George Cross by the UK and the Croix de Guerre by France for her extreme bravery.

Looking lifelike
Moss and lichen were painted on, to make the logs look old and as real as possible

Logs made of plaster were used by the SOE to smuggle arms and ammunition into enemy territory.

Lethal logs
Inside were small guns, grenades, and ammunition packed in cardboard for protection from the weather

Radio traitors

During World War II, the radio was vital for news and also for giving false information to the enemy. The Nazis used people raised in the UK to make broadcasts to the UK. One of the best known was William Joyce, who was also called Lord Haw Haw. In his radio broadcasts from Germany, he lied and told the British people that they were losing the war. Joyce was captured after the war and hanged as a traitor. Japan also used English-speaking women to broadcast to American troops. They called all of the women "Tokyo Rose."

William Joyce, who was nicknamed Lord Haw Haw because of his upper-class accent. He spoke to the British on German radio for most of World War II.

Iva Toguri D'Aquino was found guilty of being Tokyo Rose. She was later pardoned.

HOT SPOTS

British and American troops nicknamed Mildred Gillars "Axis Sally." The American-born actress spoke on Radio Berlin throughout World War II. Her best-known broadcast was just before D-Day in May 1944, when she pretended to be a mother dreaming that her son was killed as he landed in France. She was found guilty of treason and imprisoned.

Double agents

Double agents are spies who pretend to work for one country when they are really spying for an enemy power. This is a dangerous game to play, and double agents risk their lives every minute of the day.

Operation Fortitude

In 1944, the U.S., the UK, and their Allies planned to invade France. The Germans, who occupied France, were ready for the attack. But where exactly would it come? Spaniard Juan Pujol was a British double agent, and the Germans thought he was working for them. So when Pujol informed Germany that the invasion was coming in northern France, the Germans moved many of their troops there. The real invasion actually came farther south, in Normandy. When the American, British, and Canadian troops landed, the German forces were not strong enough to drive them back, and the invasion was a success.

The false information that double agent Pujol fed to the Germans was vital to the success of the Allied invasion of Normandy in 1944. This is still the largest sea-borne invasion in history.

Historic invasion
Almost three million troops crossed the English Channel from the UK to Normandy

The name's Popov

During World War II, a British naval intelligence officer named Ian Fleming met Dusko Popov, a rich, handsome spy. Popov enjoyed going to nightclubs and traveling. Years later, Ian Fleming became a writer and created a spy called Bond—James Bond—who he based on Popov. However, Popov was a double agent. He was recruited by Germany to spy on the UK but was actually handing over German secrets to the British secret service.

Identity papers belonging to Dusan "Dusko" Popov, who worked as a double agent during World War II.

The spy James Bond has been featured in many successful films. He has been played by actors who make spying appear glamorous and exciting.

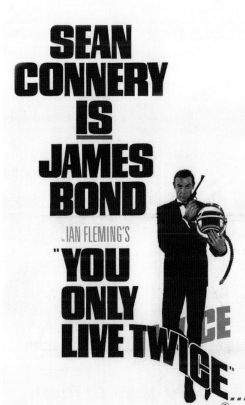

The Cold War

After World War II, the U.S. and the Soviet Union disliked each other so much that they almost started another war. The years 1947 to 1990 became known as the **Cold War**, and both sides spied on each other.

Sky-high spy

In 1960, a high-flying U.S. spy plane, called a U-2, flew over the Soviet Union to photograph its **atomic weapons**. The Soviets spotted the plane, shot it down, and captured its pilot, Gary Powers. They explained to the world that the U-2 had been spying, while the Americans pretended that Gary Powers had simply flown into Soviet territory by mistake.

The U-2 spy plane was designed to take photographs of Soviet military installations from 80,000 feet (24,000 m).

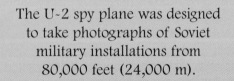

Spy on trial

Gary Powers in the dock, during his trial for spying

At his trial, Gary Powers was found guilty of espionage and sentenced to ten years in prison. However, he was freed after two years in exchange for a Soviet spy.

Harsh punishment

In 1950, the Americans uncovered a spy ring that sold atomic secrets to the Soviets. Top-secret drawings about America's atomic weapons were being passed to Julius and Ethel Rosenberg, who were U.S. citizens. They passed them on to Morton Sobell, a Russian **diplomat**. The Rosenbergs were arrested and found guilty of spying. In 1953, they were both put to death in the electric chair.

The Rosenbergs were executed, but others in the spy ring managed to escape.

Guy Burgess
Worked for the British Foreign Office

Anthony Blunt
Worked for MI5 and helped the other three spies escape

Donald Maclean
Worked for the British Foreign Office

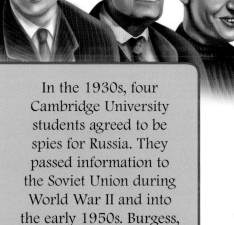

Kim Philby
Worked for MI6

In the 1930s, four Cambridge University students agreed to be spies for Russia. They passed information to the Soviet Union during World War II and into the early 1950s. Burgess, Maclean, and Philby fled to the Soviet Union just before arrest.

HOT SPOTS

During the Cold War, the German city of Berlin was divided. Half was backed by the Americans and their allies and half by the Russians and their allies. Then, in 1961, the Russians built a huge wall across the city to stop people from running away to the West. Anyone trying to escape over the wall was shot.

Tools of the trade

With spies, nothing is what it seems! They use all sorts of amazing gadgets to help them steal secrets. The CIA gives these mini-machines the nickname "sneakies."

Getting information

Scientists have invented high-tech equipment to help spies get vital information. Cameras and recorders are hidden in pens, cell phones, calculators, and eyeglasses. This allows spies to record and photograph information in secret. Then the information can be passed on through a "dead letter drop." This is an innocent-looking place where stolen information can be left to be collected later.

Mailbox? No, this is in fact a dead letter drop where stolen information can be hidden.

This pinhole camera is no bigger than a coin. Hidden in a clock, picture frame, or ornament, it spies on people at home or work.

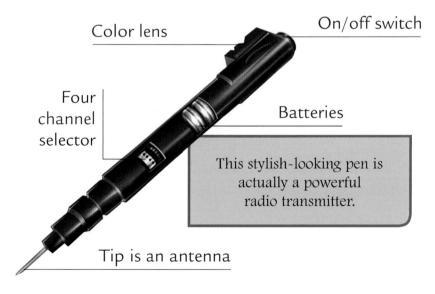

Color lens

On/off switch

Four channel selector

Batteries

This stylish-looking pen is actually a powerful radio transmitter.

Tip is an antenna

Deadly trigger
When pushed, this fired the poisoned pellet

This umbrella proved to be a deadly weapon when it was used to kill journalist Georgi Markov. A Bulgarian secret agent pressed the trigger in the handle to fire a tiny, poisoned pellet from the tip, which came out like a bullet from a gun.

Poisoned pellet
Released by the trigger

This briefcase has a hidden recorder and video. No on/off switch is needed because they work only when they detect movement.

Hollow tip
Poisoned pellet shot out from here into the victim

Innocent weapons

Spies use weapons for self-defense—and sometimes for murder. Everyday items can easily be turned into deadly weapons. Propelling pencils sprout lethal blades that slash and cut, and tiny guns can be turned into pens. The journalist Georgi Markov often criticized the Bulgarian government. So in 1978, the government decided to get rid of him. Walking in the street, Markov felt a pain in his leg as a man with an umbrella brushed past him. A few days later he was dead—killed by a poisoned pellet fired from the innocent-looking umbrella.

This average-sized, working pen is also a color video camera. It can record something more than 500 feet (150 m) away.

Spying today

Modern spying is big business. New equipment is appearing every day, available to anyone who can afford it. Businesses as well as countries spy on each other.

We can see you!

Today, space satellites are used to spy on an enemy's military bases and weapons. The powerful cameras on space satellites can photograph an object as small as a football or a human face! Almost invisible aircraft, known as **stealth planes**, are also used to find out what the enemy is up to. They are made of special materials that make it difficult for enemy radar to detect them.

Detailed photographs from a space satellite are sent back to Earth by radio.

Spy satellites can provide the intelligence services with valuable pictures of enemy military bases and missile sites. Satellites can "see" through clouds and also take pictures at night.

Bugging and hacking

Companies in all modern industries—including chemicals, fashion, cars, and cosmetics—have secret information. Their designs, plans, and formulas are worth millions of dollars and are carefully guarded. Rivals try to steal these secrets by bugging phones, installing secret cameras, and hacking into computers. They even search the trash for scraps of useful information. Another way of getting information is to pay someone who works for a company to hand over its secrets. Top workers may even be offered more money to switch jobs and work for a competitor.

HOT SPOTS

Coca-Cola has always kept its drink recipe a secret. In 2006, three people were arrested and accused of stealing its secret formula. They planned to sell it to Pepsi!

CCTV cameras are everywhere! They watch traffic, stores, homes, and businesses and are often used to help the police catch criminals.

CCTV
These special cameras can swivel from side to side

Glossary

Allies Countries that fought against Germany and Japan in World War II. The main Allies were the U.S., the UK, the Soviet Union, and France.

assassins People who murder someone, especially a political figure.

atomic weapons Nuclear bombs or warheads with great explosive power.

betray To be disloyal.

codes Systems of special symbols and letters that can be understood only by people sending and receiving a message.

Cold War The period of political conflict between the U.S. and the Soviet Union from 1945 to 1990.

concentration camp A guarded prison camp where Jews and others who were against the Nazis were imprisoned during World War II.

Confederate A member of the army of the Southern states of America, which was defeated by the North in the Civil War (1861–65).

conspiracies Secret plots or plans to carry out illegal or harmful acts.

decoded A coded message that can be read.

diplomat A person who represents a government and works peacefully with other governments.

double agent A person who pretends to work as a spy for one country while actually working as a spy for another.

espionage The act of spying to obtain secret information.

French Revolution A period of huge change in France (1789-99) when the king was overthrown and executed.

intercepting Blocking a code or message in order to decode it.

Israelites The people of Israel.

King Louis XVI King of France (1774–91). He was overthrown during the French Revolution and executed on January 21, 1793.

Napoleon Bonaparte A general during the French Revolution who later made himself Emperor of France (1804–15).

Nazi The German political party led by Adolph Hitler that controlled Germany from the early 1930s until the end of World War II.

Protestant A member of any Christian group that separated from the Roman Catholic Church.

Reign of Terror The period (September 1793–July 1794) in the French Revolution when cruel measures were taken against anyone who opposed it.

resistance fighters People who are fighting for freedom when their country is under enemy occupation.

revolutions The violent overthrow of a government or sovereign.

Revolutionary War (1775–83) The war fought because Americans wanted to be free from British rule.

Soviet Union The country, also known as the USSR, that controlled huge parts of eastern Europe and northern Asia (1922–91).

spy rings Groups of spies who work as a team, even though they may never meet.

spy satellites Machines in space that can take pictures and obtain information about objects on Earth.

stealth planes Aircraft used for espionage and designed to not be detected by enemy radar.

treason To cheat and be disloyal to one's country.

Index

Web sites

www.sciencemuseum.org.uk/visitmuseum/galleries/science_of_spying   Find out if you've got what it takes to be a modern-day spy.

www.bbc.co.uk/history/british/tudors/launch_gms_spying.shtml   Test your skills in the Elizabethan Spying Game.

www.spymuseum.org/   The site of International Spy Museum, Washington, DC.

www.cia.gov/   Find out about the Central Intelligence Agency.

www.bletchleypark.org.uk   All about Bletchley Park, the UK's National Codes Center.

www.secretcodebreaker.com   Discover the science of secret codes and ciphers.

www.bbc.co.uk/history/worldwars/wwtwo/soe_gallery_03.shtml   Some of the amazing gadgets used by the SOE during World War II.